Whole Food

39 Delicious And Nutrient-Rich Whole food Recipes

© Copyright 2016

All rights Reserved. No part of this book may be reproduced in any form without permission in writing from the author. Reviewers may quote brief passages in reviews.

Disclaimer

No part of this publication may be reproduced or transmitted in any form or by any means, mechanical or electronic, including photocopying or recording, or by any information storage and retrieval system, or transmitted by email without permission in writing from the publisher.

While all attempts have been made to verify the information provided in this publication, neither the author nor the publisher assumes any responsibility for errors, omissions or contrary interpretations of the subject matter herein.

This book is for entertainment purposes only. The views expressed are those of the author alone, and should not be taken as expert instruction or commands. The reader is responsible for his or her own actions.

Adherence to all applicable laws and regulations, including international, federal, state and local laws governing professional licensing, business practices, advertising and all other aspects of doing business in the US, Canada, UK or any other jurisdiction is the sole responsibility of the purchaser or reader.

Neither the author nor the publisher assumes any responsibility or liability whatsoever on the behalf of the purchaser or reader of these materials. Any perceived slight of any individual or organization is purely unintentional.

Contents

INTRODUCTION 6

CHAPTER 1: A BREAKFAST FIT FOR CHAMPIONS 14

1. Granola-Yogurt Parfait 14
2. Green Goddess Smoothie 15
3. Huevos Rancheros 16
4. -Grain Veggie Scramble 18
5. Zucchini Oatmeal Muffins 20
6. Homemade Granola... 22

CHAPTER 2: GUILT-FREE STARTERS & SNACKS (7 RECIPES) 24

7. Fast, Easy Guacamole 24
8. Homemade Hummus.. 26
9. Energy Bars 28
10. Snacky Balls... 30
11. Veggie Mini-Quiche 32
12. Curried Chickpea Salad Sliders 34
13. Better-Than-Frozen Pizza Pockets................... 36

CHAPTER 3: SALADS WITH SUBSTANCE 38

14. Apple-Walnut Salad with Peanut Butter-Yogurt Dressing.. 38
15. Mediterranean Bean Salad 40
16. Strawberry-Spinach Salad................................. 41
17. Summer 5-Grain Salad 42
18. Winter 5-Grain Salad 44

CHAPTER 4: SANDWICHES & WRAPS 46

19. Pocket Pita with Greek Meatballs 46
20. Make-Ahead Veggie Burrito Wraps................... 49

CHAPTER 5: SEASONAL SOUPS 51

21. SPICY WHITE BEAN & KALE SOUP 51
22. HEARTY VEGETABLE LENTIL SOUP 53
23. SUMMER GREEN PEA SOUP WITH MINT 55

CHAPTER 6: EASY ENTREES 57

24. VEGETABLE FRIED RICE...57
25. SLOW-COOKER CHICKEN...59
26. HAMBURGER SKILLET...61

CHAPTER 7: SIMPLE SIDE DISHES.....................63

27. 5-GRAIN MIX..63
28. ROASTED GARLIC SWEET POTATOES WITH QUINOA 65
29. WHOLE WHEAT BISCUITS...67

CHAPTER 8: DRESSINGS, SAUCES & SPREADS 69

30. MEDITERRANEAN DRESSING......................................69
31. CILANTRO-LIME VEGGIE SPREAD 70
32. HOMEMADE BASIL PESTO 72
33. CILANTRO-LIME PESTO WITH ARUGULA 73
34. LEMON POPPYSEED BALSAMIC DRESSING................75
35. CREAMY BASIL DRESSING 76
36. ALL-PURPOSE VINAIGRETTE......................................77

CHAPTER 9: SENSIBLE, DELECTABLE DESSERTS...78

37. PEACH PIE...78
38. SUMMERY CITRUS TART...81
39. FLOURLESS CINNAMON-PECAN COOKIES................84

CONCLUSION 86

Introduction

I want to thank you and commend you for downloading the book, "Whole Food:

39 Delicious And Nutrient-Rich Whole Food Recipes".

This book contains some of my favorite whole food recipes that have become much-loved staples at our house. They are easy to learn and offer a lot of variety, both day-to-day and season to season. Of course, rolling variations in available seasonal foods form the cornerstone of any whole food diet. That's one of the many things that set it apart from a traditional diet, which is built largely on convenience food and fast food.

More and more people are choosing to eat a diet rich in whole foods these days because of the many and wide-ranging health benefits that come with it. Eating a wide variety of foods that are as little processed as possible is the core of the definition of the term whole foods. In addition, whole foods usually refer to foods that are:

- organically grown
- both fresh and in season

- if not fresh, then either canned or frozen at home, or store-bought brands that don't use artificial additives or chemical preservatives
- as close to their natural state as possible
- sweetened with natural sweeteners such as honey and maple syrup rather than sugar, corn syrup, or artificial sweeteners

A whole food diet, much like an organic diet, prefers fresh, local ingredients that don't rely on long-distance transport, which uses unsustainable energy. But it can, and typically does, include meat, gluten, dairy, and carbs – unlike other popular diets and those which restrict specific ingredients based on allergies or weight-loss strategies.

Whole foods have been gaining in popularity for years, as evidenced by the farmer's market movement, which has exploded in the last few decades. Popular cooking shows featuring chefs who know the value and optimal flavor to be gained from fresh, seasonal produce (not to mention the cost savings) have helped spur the movement along by showing how easy it is to cook great food instead of buying packaged junk. And other clean food movements, such as vegetarianism, veganism, and the raw food movement have also coincided with the increase in whole foods popularity. Recently, corner grocers have even begun carrying organic ingredients and products, including convenience items (like frozen dinners) that mirror those favored in a traditional diet.

Perhaps, the transition to whole food has been best helped, though, by scientific studies underscoring the nutritional value and health benefits of eating diets rich in the nutrients best provided by whole food. For example, whole foods are higher in vitamins and minerals, including phytochemicals that help protect the body against chronic disease. They also contain more dietary fiber and beneficial fats as well as antioxidant phenolics and flavonoids, which have been shown to play a role in colon health, heart health, and digestive tract health.

Eating whole foods means eating a heterogeneous diet that relies on a wide variety of food sources to achieve the key benefit: combinations of nutrients from diverse sources acting synergistically to provide optimal protection against diseases of all kinds. A whole food diet can also boost energy, memory function, and physical performance. It leaves people feeling better naturally, without the need for dieting in the conventional sense. And it provides better nutrition than a traditional diet with added vitamins and dietary supplements, due largely to micronutrients that come only from plants.

Diets, as they've been known ever since doctors started recommending them – beginning with the low-calorie variety, have traditionally required measuring every serving, tracking every meal and snack, counting every calorie, and exercising like the dickens to burn it all off. This approach to food and eating turns humans into little more than machines that consume calories and produce energy – an odd way of looking at what used to be regarded as the sacred act of taking nourishment.

It's no surprise, then, that diets are so hard to stick to and so rarely succeed in the long-term. Wouldn't it be better to stop counting calories and start identifying nutrients instead?

That's exactly what I started doing, and I've never looked back. I just can't believe it took me so long to realize how programmed I was to think about food in certain ways.

For instance, I thought that counting calories would help keep me healthy. The truth is, obsessing about calories didn't make me healthy. Quite the opposite. It just made me obsessed with food, which only reminded me how hungry and unfulfilled I felt all the time. When you eat whole foods, you're much more likely to feel fuller longer and eat fewer calories overall as a result – without the need to keep tables, charts, and logs. As an added bonus, when you have healthy whole food snacks lying around the house, car, or desk, you're less likely to worry about snacking between meals because you know what you're eating is good for you.

Another myth I bought into was the notion that fast food tasted better than whole food, or that whole food tasted boring or weird. Nothing could be further from the truth. Fast food had coated my tongue, leaving my taste buds impervious to real flavor. The only thing that tasted good back when I was eating fast food was more of the same. But that changed as soon as I started eating more whole foods. Not only do whole foods have more flavor; they have better texture in most cases, too. Interestingly, the fewer processed sugars I ate, the less I craved. Soon, highly processed foods no longer tasted good to me; they tasted sweet or they tasted salty, but that's different.

Now, real food – whole, fresh, in-season foods – is what tastes good. And even my children agree. They have fast food or restaurant pizza sometimes at parties and sleepovers, and we often eat out when we drive long distances for vacations and family visits, but we've taught them that those options are just part of a bigger food landscape and that it's fine to eat them in moderation.

The last myth I believed in was that learning to eat and cook whole foods was hard or required some sort of special knowledge. I wish I had known how easy it could be to get started. It took working in a trendy little café that was known for its vegetarian and vegan offerings for me to realize how easy and simple whole food cooking could be. When I saw it and ate it every day because it was readily available and scrumptious.

And now I'd like to share some of that knowledge with you.

I hope you will enjoy the book!

Chapter 1: A Breakfast Fit For Champions

1. Granola-Yogurt Parfait

This breakfast is unbelievably easy and healthy. The kids love it!

Prep Time:

Total Time:

Serves: 2 parfait glasses

Ingredients:

2 ½ cups plain Greek yogurt

1 1/3 cup homemade granola (see recipe nr 6.)

2 cups fresh fruit (ex: sliced strawberries, blueberries, sliced kiwi)

Place 3 tablespoons yogurt in bottom of each parfait glass. Add 2 tablespoons granola and 1/3 cup fruit. Add ½ cup yogurt, followed by 2 tablespoons granola and 1/3 cup fruit. Repeat layers, and add remaining fruit on top. Serve immediately, or chill up to 30 minutes.

2. Green Goddess Smoothie

This is a power breakfast and a staple for most whole foods enthusiasts. It combines power greens with apple, lemon, ginger, and coconut for great flavor so you can start your day right without sacrificing taste.

Prep Time: 5 minutes

Cook Time: 5 minutes

Total Time: 5 minutes

Serves: 2 medium (12-ounce) smoothies or one large (24-ounce) smoothie

Ingredients:

1 unpeeled red or green apple, cored and cut into chunks

4 cups tender baby kale leaves, chopped

2 cups baby spinach leaves

juice of ½ lemon

one 1-inch knob of ginger, peeled

1/3 cup dry, unsweetened, organic coconut

1/3 cup raw walnuts

Blend all ingredients until smooth. Drink immediately.

3. Huevos Rancheros

I like to make a double batch of this when we have weekend guests. It's deceptively easy, and what a crowd-pleaser!

Prep Time: 5 minutes

Cook Time: 10 minutes

Total Time: 15 minutes

Serves: 2-3

Ingredients:

6 large eggs

3 tablespoons 1% milk

1 jalapeno, seeded and finely diced

½ cup shredded cheddar cheese

¼ cup fresh salsa

2 tablespoons guacamole **(see nr 7 for my easy, fast recipe,)**

1 tablespoon plain Greek yogurt

cilantro

Crack eggs into medium bowl. Add milk and whisk until well combined. Stir in jalapeno, and pour into skillet. Cook on medium heat, pushing cooked egg to center as it cooks and allowing liquid egg mixture to fall to the edges. Flip over in sections when nearly cooked through, and top with cheese. Cook two minutes longer, and remove from heat. Add remaining toppings, and serve.

4.-Grain Veggie Scramble

This is the perfect vegan substitute to an egg-based breakfast.

Prep Time: 10 minutes

Cook Time: 10 minutes

Total Time: 20 minutes

Serves: 1-2

Ingredients:

2 tablespoons avocado or coconut oil

2 stalks celery, diced

½ small onion, diced

½ cup diced ham, bacon, or vegan meat alternative

2 cups 5-grain mix, cooked and drained

¾ teaspoon dried basil

¼ teaspoon dried thyme

½ teaspoon sea salt

¼ teaspoon freshly ground black pepper

½ cup shredded cheddar cheese or vegan alternative

Sauté celery and onion in oil over medium-high heat. Add meat (or meat alternative), 5-grain mix, and seasonings. Stir well and cook 5 minutes. Top with cheese and serve warm.

5. Zucchini Oatmeal Muffins

I guarantee these are the best thing you'll ever take camping! I made a double batch once and still ran out before the weekend was through. Highly popular with hungry teens, these muffins will keep them full for hours.

Prep Time: 20 minutes

Cook Time: 15 minutes

Total Time: 35 minutes

Serves: 2 dozen

Ingredients:

2 ½ cups whole wheat flour

1 cup chopped walnuts

½ cup rolled oats

1 tablespoon baking powder

1 teaspoon sea salt

1 teaspoon ground cinnamon

4 eggs

1 ½ cups real maple syrup

one medium zucchini (about 10 oz.), grated

¾ cup coconut oil

Preheat oven to 400°.

Line 24 muffin cups with paper liners, or spray with cooking oil.

In a large bowl, measure the first six ingredients. In a medium bowl, beat eggs slightly. Stir in maple syrup, zucchini, and oil. Poor into flour mixture and stir only until moist. Batter will be lumpy. Fill muffin cups ¾ full.

Bake 15 minutes, or until tops are beginning to brown.

6. Homemade Granola

Granola makes a wonderful breakfast when combined with plain Greek yogurt or 1% milk, but it can also double as a topping *for fruit crisps or eaten as a snack.*

Prep Time: 15 minutes

Cook Time: 25 minutes

Total Time: 40 minutes

Serves: about 6 cups

Ingredients:

4 cups rolled oats

½ cup pepitas

½ cup chopped walnuts

½ cup cashew pieces or mixed nuts

1 teaspoon sea salt

½ teaspoon ground cinnamon

½ cup coconut oil, melted

½ cup maple syrup

1 teaspoon vanilla extract

2/3 cup sun-dried raisins

¾ cup unsweetened shredded coconut

Preheat oven to 350°

Line a bar pan with parchment paper. In a large bowl combine rolled oats, nuts, seasonings, and oil. Mix until well coated. Add maple syrup and vanilla extract. Stir thoroughly and pour into pan, spreading to ensure even baking. Bake 20-25 minutes, stirring about halfway through. Cool completely. Then add raisins and coconut. Mix to combine. Store in airtight container.

Chapter 2: Guilt-Free Starters & Snacks (7 recipes)

7. Fast, Easy Guacamole

Ripe avocados are soft when you press your thumb into the bottom. When you pop off the stem, it should appear white or green, not brown or black.

Prep Time: 10 minutes

Chill Time: 20 minutes

Total Time: 30 minutes

Serves: about 2 ½ cups

Ingredients:

2 ripe avocados, diced

¼ cup white onion, minced

juice of one lime

¾ cup packed cilantro leaves, chopped fine

1 small tomato, seeded and diced

Combine all ingredients except tomato in a small bowl. Mash with potato masher to desired consistency. Stir in tomato and chill 20 minutes. Garnish with additional cilantro leaves and a lime wedge and serve immediately, or seal with plastic wrap and store in fridge up to 48 hours. Avocado will begin to brown immediately. Press plastic down onto the surface to reduce browning.

8. Homemade Hummus

Ever since I got my food processor, I can't stop coming up with new ideas for different flavors of hummus. What flavor combinations can you think of?

Prep Time: 10 minutes

Cook Time: 10 minutes

Total Time: 10 minutes

Ingredients:

2 cups chickpeas, cooked, drained, and rinsed

2 tablespoons high-quality extra-virgin olive oil

2 tablespoons tahini

juice of one medium lemon, or more to taste

2 cloves garlic, chopped

¼ cup water

½ teaspoon sea salt

jalapenos, roasted red pepper, black olives, or other garnish

Blend all ingredients together in food processor, adding water as needed to make a thick paste. Transfer to bowl. Place in fridge and chill 30-60 minutes or until ready to serve, up to one week. Just before serving, add a drizzle of olive oil and garnish as desired. Serve with feta cheese and whole-wheat pita toast points.

9. Energy Bars

These energy-packed bars are a staple at our house and provide a healthy alternative to store-bought granola bars.

Prep Time: 10 minutes

Total Time: 10 minutes

Serves: 8

Ingredients:

2 cups cashew nuts or pieces

2 cups Medjool dates, pitted and minced

1 cup almonds

2 tablespoons toasted flax seeds

1 tablespoon pure vanilla extract

Pinch of sea salt

2/3 cup unsweetened flaked coconut

Line an 8x8 or 9x9 pan with parchment paper.

Combine first six ingredients in food processor and pulse until a thick paste is formed. Add coconut and process until mixture is smooth and forms a thick dough. (2-3 tablespoons of water may be added if needed to achieve desired consistency.)

Turn dough out into parchment-lined pan and spread evenly, pressing into edges and corners as needed. Chill one hour and then cut into 2-inch x 4-inch bars.

10. Snacky Balls

These tasty treats sit in the fridge until I need a pick-me-up or late-night snack. This recipe is great for experimentation. The kids like to add miniature chocolate chips, and I like to roll mine in flax seeds.

Prep Time: 10 minutes

Total Time: 10 minutes

Serves: about 12-15 balls

Ingredients:

1 ½ cups nuts or 1 cup nut flour or meal

8-10 Medjool dates

1 cup shredded organic coconut

2 tablespoons honey

3-4 tablespoons water, if needed

2 tablespoons chia seeds, sesame seeds, or flax seeds (optional)

Line a glass pan with parchment paper and chill in fridge.

Combine nut meal and dates in food processor and pulse until combined. Add honey and coconut and blend until smooth. Add water if needed. Mixture will be sticky and should form a stiff dough.

Form into balls and roll in seeds, if desired. Drop onto prepared pan. Cover and chill. Keeps about 10-14 days in the fridge before drying out. Freezes well.

11. Veggie Mini-Quiche

These savory little treats are ideal for parties, but can also be frozen and reheated as needed for a quick breakfast on the go. Try adding jalapenos for a spicy kick.

Prep Time: 20 minutes

Cook Time: 22 minutes

Total Time: 45 minutes

Serves: 24 individual quiches

Ingredients:

whole wheat pie crust for double-crust pie (see recipe, page)

½ cup 1% milk

2 eggs

½ cup zucchini, finely chopped

½ cup broccoli, finely chopped

1 green onion, white and green parts, minced

1 clove garlic, minced

¼ teaspoon sea salt

dash of freshly ground black pepper

½ cup shredded cheddar cheese

1 tablespoon whole wheat flour

Preheat oven to 375°

Line mini-muffin pan with paper liners or grease with coconut oil. In a medium bowl, whisk together eggs and milk. Add veggies and seasonings. Toss cheese with flour and fold in gently.

On a lightly floured surface, roll out half of dough (one disc) to a thickness of ¼ inch. Using biscuit cutter or inverted drinking glass, cut 12 circles. Gently press each circle into mini-muffin pan, ensuring sides of each crust rise above pan edge. Repeat with second crust.

Fill each crust with approximately 1 tablespoon of egg mixture. Bake 17-22 minutes, or until crusts are light golden brown and quiches are set. Cool in pan 5 minutes before removing. Serve immediately, refrigerate for up to one week, or freeze for up to 6 months.

To reheat from frozen, preheat oven or toaster oven to 375°. Bake 10-12 minutes or until heated through.

12. Curried Chickpea Salad Sliders

These are perfect on game day, but really they're great anytime, especially for entertaining.

Prep Time: 15 minutes

Total Time: 15 minutes

Serves: 8 sliders

Ingredients:

1 ½ cups cooked chickpeas, drained and rinsed

1 small avocado, cut into cubes

1 tablespoon tahini

¼ teaspoon minced garlic

¼ cup diced red onion

½ cup chopped cilantro

¼ cup chopped walnuts

½ teaspoon curry powder, or to taste

juice of one small lemon

sea salt and fresh ground black pepper

8 slider buns

lettuce, tomato, onion, pickles, etc. as desired for toppings

Combine chickpeas, avocado, tahini, garlic, curry powder, lemon with some salt and pepper in a medium bowl. Mash together with a potato masher until combined. Stir in onion, cilantro, and walnuts, and season to taste. Assemble sandwiches hot, or chill mixture until ready to serve (up to one day).

13. Better-Than-Frozen Pizza Pockets

These are a big game day favorite that can also be baked halfway and frozen for an easy-to-reheat pocket pizza later on.

Prep Time: 45 minutes

Cook Time: 15 minutes

Total Time: one hour

Serves: 6

Ingredients:

Dough

    1 cup *warm* water

    2 teaspoons dry active yeast

    1 teaspoon salt

    2 tablespoons olive oil*

    2 ¾ cup whole wheat flour

Filling

    1 ½ cup Spaghetti Sauce or Homemade Basil Pesto **(nr 32)** or Cilantro-Lime Pesto with Arugula **(nr 33)**

    1 ¼ cup shredded mozzarella cheese

    2/3 cup Parmesan cheese

Preheat oven to 450º

Make dough: Add yeast to warm water and let rest one minute. When a foam appears, add salt and oil. Stir gently. In a food processor with a dough hook, combine yeast mixture with flour and process until a dough forms. Coat a clean bowl with olive oil*. Transfer dough into bowl and coat with oil. Cover with plastic wrap and a clean towel. Let rest 25 minutes.

Meanwhile, mix together ingredients for filling.

Divide dough into 6 equal parts and form into balls. Roll each ball out into a square and add ½ cup filling. Bring edges together and seal with water. Place on ungreased baking sheet with seams down. Cut slits in tops of each pizza pocket to vent steam. Dust with additional parmesan cheese, or brush with egg white wash and sprinkle with raw sesame seeds, if desired.

Bake 12-15 minutes or until tops are golden brown and sauce is beginning to bubble up over steam vents. Cool 10 minutes and serve with additional sauce.

*Olive oil is highly processed and something I usually avoid. However, for pizza dough it is the best option.

Chapter 3: Salads With Substance

14. Apple-Walnut Salad with Peanut Butter-Yogurt Dressing

This fall favorite can be served for breakfast, as a side dish for lunch or dinner, or even as dessert. It's easy, versatile, and oh-so-yummy!

Prep Time: 10 minutes

Total Time: 10 minutes

Serves: 4-6 ½-cup servings

Ingredients:

2 medium apples (tart or green apples work best), cored and diced

1 cup plain Greek yogurt

½ cup creamy peanut butter

2 tablespoons maple syrup

½ cup walnuts

¼ cup sun-dried raisins

Toss all ingredients together in bowl. Serve immediately, or chill for up to 24 hours. Stir before serving.

15. Mediterranean Bean Salad

This is the perfect side dish to accompany one of our summer favorites, Pita Pockets with Greek Meatballs.

Prep Time: 15 minutes

Total Time: 15 minutes

Serves: 4-6

Ingredients:

cut kernels (raw) from one ear of sweet corn

2 cups dark red kidney beans, cooked, drained, and rinsed

¼ cup minced red onion

one medium tomato, chopped

2 tablespoons fresh Italian parsley, chopped

Mediterranean dressing (recipe below)

Combine ingredients in medium bowl and toss with ½ cup **Mediterranean dressing (Nr 30).**

16. Strawberry-Spinach Salad

This salad is so delectable, my kids have actually asked for it for dessert!

Prep Time: 20 minutes

Total Time: 20 minutes

Serves: 4-6

Ingredients:

1 lb. fresh spinach

1 pint strawberries, cleaned and sliced

2 oz. slivered almonds, toasted

1-1 ½ cups All Purpose Vinaigrette **(see recipe, nr 36)**

Wash spinach and remove stems. Place into large salad bowl. Clean and slice strawberries, and add to spinach. Toast slivered almonds *lightly* in toaster oven, or on stovetop in a dry skillet over medium heat. Almonds will burn easily. Add almonds to spinach and strawberries, and pour vinaigrette over the top. Toss and serve promptly.

17. Summer 5-Grain Salad

Once you learn to make this salad, you won't believe how many combinations you can come up with! Use whatever veggies and fruits are available in your area. Summer *salad is always yummiest when made with fresh, local ingredients.*

Prep Time: 10 minutes

Total Time: 10 minutes

Serves: 8 cups

Ingredients:

½ cup celery, chopped

½ cup green onion, chopped

½ cup carrots, chopped

1 cup grape tomatoes, halved

½ cup fresh green beans, blanched and cut into 1-inch pieces

½ cup fresh spinach, sliced into thin strips

½ cup fresh baby kale, sliced into thin strips

8 cups 5-grain mix, cooked and cooled **(see recipe, nr 27)**

1-1 ½ cups All-Purpose Vinaigrette **(see recipe, nr 36)** or other salad dressing

Combine all ingredients in large mixing bowl and stir thoroughly. Salad stores well in fridge up to 5-7 days. Always stir well before serving, as dressing may settle to the bottom.

18. Winter 5-Grain Salad

The winter version of my favorite summer salad relies on frozen, rather than fresh vegetables, and adds nuts and boiled eggs to make for a heartier cold salad. It makes a perfect side dish for sandwiches and soups.

Prep Time: 10 minutes

Total Time: 10 minutes

Serves: 8 cups

Ingredients:

½ cup diced celery

½ cup diced carrot

½ cup white onion, chopped

½ cup frozen green beans, blanched and cut into 1-inch pieces

two boiled eggs, peeled and chopped

1 cup almonds, cashews, or mixed nuts

8 cups 5-grain mix, cooked and cooled **(see recipe, nr 27)**

1-1 ½ cups All Purpose Vinaigrette **(see recipe, nr 36)** or other salad dressing

Combine all ingredients in large mixing bowl and stir well. Serve immediately or store in fridge up to 5-7 days. Always stir well before serving.

Chapter 4: Sandwiches & Wraps

19. Pocket Pita with Greek Meatballs

I use ground beef for these Greek meatballs, but you can use lamb, turkey, or meat substitute, if you prefer. We like to eat these throughout the summer, so I make the meatballs ahead of time and freeze them. They reheat nicely in the toaster oven, which reduces heat in the kitchen while helping us save money on our energy bill.

Prep Time: 45 minutes

Cook Time: 10-12 minutes

Total Time: about an hour

Serves: 4

Ingredients:

spray cooking oil

4 whole-grain pita breads

½ cup low-fat (1%) milk

¾ pound lean, grass-fed, local ground beef

3 tablespoons grated red onion

¾ teaspoon dried oregano

¼ teaspoon ground allspice

¼ teaspoon freshly ground black pepper

½ teaspoon fine sea salt, divided

¾ cup (six ounces) Greek yogurt

½ cup peeled, minced cucumber

1 tablespoon freshly squeezed lemon juice

1 tomato, finely diced

1 cup shredded romaine lettuce

Preheat oven to 425°. Spray oil on small baking sheet.

Cut the top 1/3 off of each pita. Separate them, and tear two of them into small pieces and place in bowl, reserving the other two for another use. Cover with milk and let soak until soft, about 15 minutes.

Meanwhile, combine ground beef, onion, oregano, allspice, pepper, and ½ teaspoon of the salt in a medium bowl. Remove pita from milk, squeezing gently to remove excess liquid; add to beef mixture. Mix until well combined.

Form the mixture into 16 balls of roughly the same size. Place on baking sheet and bake 10-12 minutes, giving the pan a good shake halfway through to ensure even cooking.

Meanwhile, combine yogurt, cucumber, and lemon juice in a small bowl. Set aside.

To assemble, fill each pita, starting with tomato and lettuce. Then add four meatballs. Spoon yogurt sauce on top and serve immediately.

Otherwise, cool meatballs completely and freeze. To reheat, place in toaster oven on center rack at 400° for 20 to 25 minutes, or until dark brown on the outside and heated through.

20. Make-Ahead Veggie Burrito Wraps

We make a batch of these and throw them in the cooler before a road trip. They hold together well and taste wonderful, even cold. We eat them when we don't want to eat "fast food" or anytime we're going to be without any healthy food options.

Prep Time: 30 minutes

Total Time: 30 minutes

Serves: 6 burritos

Ingredients:

6 whole wheat tortillas, lightly steamed*

3 cups Red Beans and Rice or Unforgettable Refried Beans or Black Bean & Corn Taco Filling

12 ounces shredded cheddar cheese

2/3 cup guacamole

2/3 cup fresh salsa

2/3 cup plain Greek yogurt

hot sauce, minced jalapenos, and cilantro (optional)

Starting with chilled or room-temperature beans, fill each tortilla with ½ cup bean mixture, 2 ounces cheese, 1 tablespoon each of guacamole, salsa, and yogurt. Top with hot sauce, peppers, or cilantro. Wrap tightly from edge, tucking ends in as you go. Seal edges of tortilla with a little water and wrap in foil. Can be eaten immediately or stored in fridge or cooler up to 2 days.

*To steam tortillas, remove center piece from vegetable steamer. Place into 12-inch skillet with one inch water in the bottom. Heat to boiling and place tortilla in basket, flipping with tongs after 30-60 seconds and steaming the other side. Turn heat to low and steam each tortilla as you need it. Do not over steam.

Chapter 5: Seasonal Soups

21. Spicy White Bean & Kale Soup

This soup is unbelievably easy to make and warms us right up on a rainy or snowy day.

Prep Time: 5 minutes

Cook Time: 15 minutes

Total Time: 20 minutes

Serves: 4-6 servings

Ingredients:

1 tablespoon olive oil

1 sweet onion, minced

1 stock celery, chopped

2 medium carrots, chopped

2 cloves garlic, minced

2 cups stewed tomatoes

2 quarts vegetable broth

2 cups cooked and drained white cannellini beans

½ teaspoon dried oregano

½ teaspoon dried thyme

¼ teaspoon cayenne pepper

½ teaspoon sea salt

¼ teaspoon ground black pepper

2 cups shredded kale

¼ cup fresh Italian parsley, chopped

Extra-virgin olive oil and grated Parmesan cheese, for garnish (optional)

In Large stock pot, heat oil over medium heat. Add onion, celery, carrots, and garlic. Sauté 5 minutes, or until onion is translucent, but not brown. Add tomatoes, broth, beans, and seasonings, and bring to a boil. Cover and reduce heat to medium-low. Simmer 10 minutes. Add kale and cook 3-5 minutes more, until tender. Garnish with chopped parsley, olive oil, and Parmesan cheese.

22. Hearty Vegetable Lentil Soup

This soup works just as well with frozen veggies in the winter time as it does with fresh vegetables on a rainy summer night.

Prep Time: 10 minutes

Cook Time: 20 minutes

Total Time: 30 minutes

Serves:

Ingredients:

2 stalks celery, diced

1 medium onion, diced

3 tablespoons cold-pressed grape seed oil

1 cup diced carrots

2 cups diced tomato, fresh or stewed

1 cup green lentils

½ cup green peas, fresh or frozen

½ cup corn kernels, fresh or frozen

2 tablespoons dried basil

1 teaspoon dried thyme

½ teaspoon marjoram

½ teaspoon cayenne pepper

½ teaspoon smoked paprika

2 small bay leaves

2 teaspoons sea salt

1 teaspoon freshly ground black pepper

1 teaspoon freshly squeezed lemon juice

1 tablespoon honey

5 small potatoes, diced

4 cups vegetable stock plus water

In a large stock pot, sauté celery and onion in oil until soft. Add garlic and sauté one minute more. Add stock, vegetables, and seasonings and stir. Bring to a boil. Cover and reduce heat to simmer on medium-low for 20-25 minutes, stirring occasionally. Add water as needed.

23. Summer Green Pea Soup with Mint

This cold soup is perfect for summer nights and goes nicely with a tall glass of iced tea and a handful of multigrain crackers with organic cheese slices.

Prep Time: 10 minutes plus 2 hours

Cook Time: 30 minutes

Total Time: 40 minutes plus 2 hours

Serves: 4-6

Ingredients:

2 tablespoons olive oil

1 medium onion, chopped

1 white Japanese yam, peeled and chopped

1 leek, both white and green parts, chopped

1 quart vegetable broth (or chicken broth) plus 2 cups water (or 6 cups water)

Couple pinches sea salt, to taste

3 cups freshly shelled garden peas (or one 12 ounce package of frozen peas, defrosted)

1 cup fresh mint leaves, chopped

Raw cashew "sour cream," tofu "sour cream," or crème fraîche for garnish (optional)

2 tablespoons chives, chopped fine

Heat oil in large pot over medium heat. Add onions, yam, and leeks, and cook 5-7 minutes, until onion is *beginning* to soften. Add broth, water, and sea salt and bring to a boil. Cover and reduce heat to simmer.

Cook 20 minutes or until the vegetables are tender. Remove from heat and let cool slightly (*about* 10-15 minutes). When still hot, but no longer boiling, add the peas and mint leaves. Allow to cool to room temperature.

Transfer soup mixture to *blender* and purée. Adjust the seasoning as needed and pour soup into a bowl. Chill in fridge two hours.

Serve with crème fraîche (or substitute) and chives.

Chapter 6: Easy Entrees
24. Vegetable Fried Rice

This is a fast side dish and a great way to use up leftover rice. You can also add meat or seafood if you'd like.

Prep Time: 15 minutes

Cook Time: 10 minutes

Total Time: 25 minutes

Serves: 4

Ingredients:

4 tablespoons avocado oil or coconut oil

¼ cup diced onion

¼ cup diced celery

¼ cup diced carrot

4 cups cooked organic brown rice

3 cloves garlic, minced

2 eggs

1 teaspoon sea salt

½ teaspoon freshly ground black pepper

1 tablespoon honey

¼ cup soy sauce

1 teaspoon sesame seed oil

sesame seeds, scallions, and freshly squeezed lemon juice for garnish

Heat oil in large wok. Add onion, celery, carrot, and tofu. Sauté until vegetables are soft and tofu is browned on all sides. Add rice and stir. Add garlic and toss with rice mixture. Cook two minutes. Push all ingredients two sides of wok, and crack eggs in middle. Scramble eggs and cook four minutes longer. Toss cooked eggs together with rice mixture and season with salt and pepper. Remove from heat and add honey, soy sauce, and sesame seed oil. Toss again to coat. Garnish with sesame seeds, green onion, and lemon juice.

25. Slow-Cooker Chicken

The easiest way to cook a whole bird. Serve it with whole wheat pasta and Parmesan *cheese or use for Tortilla Soup* **(see recipe, page)**

Prep Time:

Cook Time:

Total Time:

Serves:

Ingredients:

1 whole chicken, cleaned (giblets removed) with skin

Dry rub:

>1 tablespoon dried basil
>
>1 teaspoon dried thyme
>
>½ teaspoon garlic powder
>
>½ teaspoon onion powder
>
>½ teaspoon sea salt
>
>¼ teaspoon ground coriander
>
>¼ teaspoon tarragon
>
>¼ teaspoon freshly ground black pepper
>
>dash of cayenne pepper

Clean chicken and pat dry. Mix seasonings together and rub on chicken (inside and out). Place 2 bay leaves in bottom of slow cooker and transfer chicken on top. Cover and cook on low, 5-6 hours. Chicken will add its own broth, so no need to add any liquid.

26. Hamburger Skillet

For an interesting twist, add 2 tablespoons Madras Curry along with the milk and vegetables.

Prep Time: 10 minutes

Cook Time: 20 minutes

Total Time: 30 minutes

Serves: 4

Ingredients:

1 lb. lean, grass-fed ground beef

¼ cup white onion, diced

¼ cup celery, diced

1 teaspoon sea salt

½ teaspoon freshly ground black pepper

¼ cup chopped carrots

¼ cup fresh or frozen peas

2 cups diced tomato, fresh or stewed

2 ½ cups 1% milk

¾ cup Parmesan cheese

¼ teaspoon dried thyme

½ teaspoon dried basil

½ pound whole-wheat pasta tubes or spirals

Brown meat with onion, celery salt, and pepper in skillet. Add vegetables, milk, cheese, and *seasonings* and stir well. Add pasta and bring to a boil. Reduce heat, cover, and simmer 10-12 minutes, or until pasta is al dente and liquid is mostly absorbed. Stir and remove from heat. Cover and let sit an additional five minutes. Sauce will thicken as it cools.

Chapter 7: Simple Side Dishes

27. 5-Grain Mix

This easy mix of whole grains, which I make in advance and store all week, provides an easy answer to a healthy side dish, adds bulk to salads, and can substitute for white rice in just about any application. I even used it in place of eggs to turn an omelet into a vegan scramble when necessary.

Prep Time: 5 minutes

Cook Time: 50 minutes

Total Time: 55 minutes

Serves: 6-8 cups

Ingredients:

2 cups whole grains, made up of roughly equal parts:

> hard red wheat berries
>
> hard white wheat berries
>
> spelt
>
> kamut
>
> wild rice

8-10 cups water, vegetable stock, or chicken stock

2 teaspoons sea salt

In a large stock pot, bring water and sea salt to a boil. Meanwhile, rinse whole grains under clear water, picking through and cleaning as needed. When the water begins to boil, add the grains and stir. Return to boil; cover, and reduce heat to a simmer. Boil on med-low heat, 45 to 50 minutes, stirring occasionally. Add boiling (or *very* hot) water if water level gets too low.

Test for doneness by removing a few kernels and letting them cool before tasting. Grains should spring back when bitten, but not be hard to chew. If needed, continue boiling 5-10 minutes longer. Drain and allow to cool before storing in fridge up to seven days, or season as desired and use immediately.

28. Roasted Garlic Sweet Potatoes with Quinoa

The roasted garlic is a cornerstone of this family favorite, which keeps evolving whenever we come up with new ideas. You could swap red potatoes for the sweet potatoes and green beans for the peas, if you like. Or try a combination of russet potatoes and carrots. The possibilities are endless.

Prep Time: 5 minutes

Cook Time: 50 minutes

Total Time: 55 minutes

Serves: 5-6

Ingredients:

3 sweet potatoes, peeled and cut into 1-inch cubes

1 medium onion, quartered

12 cloves garlic, peeled and crushed

1 tablespoon olive oil

½ teaspoon sea salt, or to taste

¼ teaspoon ground black pepper

1 cup uncooked quinoa

2 cups water

1 cup fresh or frozen green peas

Salt to taste

2 cups cooked, drained chickpeas

¼ cup green onion, chopped

Preheat oven to 425°. Stir together garlic, potatoes, onions, oil, salt, and pepper in large baking dish and *roast* for 40-50 minutes, stirring 2-3 times.

Meanwhile, combine water, quinoa, peas, and salt in a medium saucepan. Bring to a boil. Cover and simmer until water is absorbed, about 10 minutes. Add cooked *chickpeas* and stir.

Mix together quinoa *and* potato mixtures, and garnish with green onion.

29. Whole Wheat Biscuits

These are wonderful additions to any hot breakfast, Sunday dinner, or family meal, but they are best eaten on day one. They can double as shortcakes for strawberry shortcake in case you need to get rid of a bunch of them quickly.

Prep Time: 20 minutes

Cook Time: 12 minutes

Total Time: 30-35 minutes

Serves: 1 dozen

Ingredients:

2 cups whole wheat flour

4 teaspoons baking powder

½ teaspoon sea salt

3 tablespoons coconut oil, room temperature or colder

¾ – 1 cup 1% milk

Sift together flour, baking powder, and sea salt. Add cold coconut oil and blend with pastry *blender* or cut with knife. When mixture is well blended, add milk all at once. Mix gently, as overworking the dough will turn biscuits dense.

Turn out onto floured surface. Knead 20-30 times. Roll to about ¾ inch and cut with *biscuit* cutter or inverted drinking glass. Bake on ungreased cookie sheet 12 minutes, or until tops begin to brown.

Chapter 8: Dressings, Sauces & Spreads

30. Mediterranean Dressing

Prep Time: 5 minutes

Total Time: 5 minutes

Serves: 1 1/3 cup

Ingredients:

4-5 cloves garlic, chopped or pressed

1/3 cup fresh lemon juice

1 cup extra virgin olive oil

sea salt and pepper to taste

Press or chop garlic and combine with lemon juice. Drizzle and olive oil while whisking constantly. Add sea salt and pepper to taste. Use immediately or store in fridge for up to 10 days.

31. Cilantro-Lime Veggie Spread

This spread goes on everything, and hides ton of nutrients under generous flavors.

Prep Time: 5 minutes

Total Time: 5 minutes

Serves:

Ingredients:

½ cup steamed, shelled edamame

1 medium carrot, grated

1 cup spinach leaves

½ cup cilantro

juice and zest of one lime

1 tablespoon minced shallots

1 clove garlic

1 tablespoon honey

¾ teaspoon sea salt

3 tablespoons coconut oil

3-4 tablespoons water

Place all ingredients except water and coconut oil into a food processor and pulse until a mixture begins to form. Add coconut oil and continue processing until smooth. Add water as needed until purée reaches the desired consistency. Chill until ready to use, up to 48 hours.

32. Homemade Basil Pesto

I like to preserve the freshness of the garden all year round by making big batches of this stuff in the summer and freezing it for the winter. Spoon it into ice cube trays and freeze before popping out into a plastic bag for storage and easy measuring.

Prep Time: 10 minutes

Total Time: 10 minutes

Serves: 1 ½ cups

Ingredients:

2 cups packed fresh basil leaves

2-3 cloves garlic

¼-1/3 cup pine nuts or walnuts

½-2/3 cup flax seed oil

½ cup grated Parmesan cheese

sea salt and freshly ground black pepper

Combine basil, garlic, nuts, and cheese in bowl of a food processor and pulse until the mixture reaches a fine paste. Drizzle in flax seed oil until the pesto reaches the desired consistency.

33. Cilantro-Lime Pesto With Arugula

I love the peppery taste of arugula, and was thrilled to find a pesto recipe that would allow me to preserve the flavor of arugula for sandwiches, pasta, and whole grain salads before it goes bad.

Prep Time: 10 minutes

Total Time: 10 minutes

Serves: 1 ½ cups

Ingredients:

1 clove garlic, peeled and halved

zest of ½ lime, finely grated

½ teaspoon ground coriander

1/3 cup chopped walnuts

½ cup Parmesan cheese, finely grated

2 cups packed arugula leaves

½ cup packed cilantro leaves

2/3 cup flax seed oil

generous squeeze of fresh lime juice

sea salt and freshly ground black pepper

In food processor, combine all ingredients except oil. Pulse until mixture reaches a fine paste. On a low setting, drizzle in olive oil until desired texture is reached. Pesto can be used immediately, refrigerated for up to one week, or frozen for up to one year.

34. Lemon Poppyseed Balsamic Dressing

Use this dressing over green salads and blanched vegetables for a spark of flavor that will bring life to any ordinary meal.

Prep Time: 10 minutes

Total Time: 10 minutes

Serves: 2 cups

Ingredients:

¼ cup white balsamic vinegar

¼ cup fresh squeezed lemon juice

1 cup extra virgin olive oil

2 tablespoons poppy seeds

½ teaspoon dry mustard

¼ teaspoon cayenne pepper

½ teaspoon sea salt

¼ teaspoon freshly ground black pepper

Stir together vinegar and lemon juice. Add seasonings, and whisk in olive oil. Serve immediately or store in fridge up to one week. Oil will solidify in fridge and must be brought up to room temperature before using.

35. Creamy Basil Dressing

If you like basil pesto, you'll love this creamy basil dressing. Thin it down with a little bit of extra virgin olive oil to use on spinach salad, or use as-is on summer pasta, or sandwiches.

Prep Time: 10 minutes

Total Time: 10 minutes

Serves: about 2 cups

Ingredients:

¾ cup fresh basil

½ cup extra-virgin olive oil

¼ cup fresh squeezed lemon juice

½ teaspoon garlic, minced

1 cup plain Greek yogurt

¼ cup hummus **(see recipe, nr 8)**

Mince basil and set aside. In large bowl, stir together hummus, Greek yogurt, lemon juice, and garlic. Drizzle in olive oil, whisking to combine thoroughly. Add minced basil and stir. Use immediately or store in fridge up to one week.

36. All-Purpose Vinaigrette

This salad dressing is versatile and easy to make, so I use it on everything.

Prep Time: 5 minutes

Total Time: 5 minutes

Serves: 1 ½ cups

Ingredients:

1 cup extra virgin olive oil

½ cup apple cider vinegar

½ teaspoon smoked paprika

1 tablespoon minced shallots

½ cup honey

dash cayenne pepper

dash freshly ground black pepper

Thoroughly whisk or shake ingredients together and use immediately.

Chapter 9: Sensible, Delectable Desserts

37. Peach Pie

A summer favorite – we love it with fresh peaches from our local farmers market. My family eats it so often that I make big batches of the filling and can them for use year-round.

Prep Time: 30 minutes

Cook Time: 75 minutes

Total Time: One hour 45 minutes

Serves: One 9-inch pie

Ingredients:

Crust:

2 ½ cups whole wheat pastry flour

2 tablespoons maple syrup

½ teaspoon sea salt

1 cup cold unsalted organic butter

6-8 tablespoons cold water

2 teaspoons lemon juice

Filling:

3 ½ cups sliced fresh peaches

juice and zest of one lemon

½ cup honey

1/3 cup organic fruit (grape or cherry) juice

3 tablespoons whole wheat flour

1/8 teaspoon ground cinnamon

1/8 teaspoon almond extract

Preheat oven to 375 °

Mix together ingredients for filling and set aside.

Mix together flour, sugar, and salt. Cut in butter with pastry cutter until mixture forms balls the size of *small* peas. Stir together water and lemon juice, and sprinkle over flour mixture one tablespoon at a time. Toss with fork and pushed to side of bowl, repeating until a dough has formed. Press dough into ball and divide in two. Form each half into a disc and cover in plastic. Let rest for 30 minutes in refrigerator.

On a lightly floured surface, roll each disc into an 11-inch circle. Transfer the first to a 9-inch pie plate and trim excess dough, leaving a 1-inch overhang. Add filling and top with second crust. Crimp the two crusts together and flute the edges. Cut several long slits in the top crust before baking.

Bake 75 minutes, or until crust is golden brown and juices are beginning to bubble over the top of the slits.

38. Summery Citrus Tart

This refreshing dessert has the sweet, tart zing of citrus to perfectly cap off any summer meal. Garnish with fresh mint leaves for an even brighter flavor, or add crème fraîche and orange slices to modernize a classical presentation.

Prep Time: 25 minutes

Cook Time: 20 minutes

Total Time: 55 minutes

Serves: 6-8

Ingredients:

Crust:

1 ½ cups almond flour

1 pinch of sea salt

¼ teaspoon baking soda

½ teaspoon ground cardamom

1 teaspoon pure vanilla extract

3 tablespoons coconut oil

1 tablespoon maple syrup

1 tablespoon water

Curd:

two thirds cup honey

juice of one lemon

juice of one orange

2 large eggs

2 large egg yolks

grated zest from one lemon

grated zest from one orange

4 tablespoons unsalted organic butter

Preheat oven to 350°

Pulse together in food processor the almond flour, sea salt, baking soda, and cardamom. In a bowl, stir together vanilla, coconut oil, maple syrup, and water. Slowly add the wet ingredients to the dry and continue to pulse dough until thoroughly combined. Transfer into tart pan and press uniformly across the bottom all the way to the edges.

Bake 18-20 minutes, or until crust is golden brown. *Do not overbake*. Remove from oven and allow to cool completely.

Meanwhile, whisk together in a 1-quart saucepan the sugar, juice, egg yolks, and eggs. Cook over low heat until sugar is completely dissolved and the curd begins to simmer. Increase heat to medium and whisk in butter. Cook, stirring constantly, until mixture begins to thicken, about 10 to 12 minutes. When it resembles the consistency of putting, remove from heat and add lemon zest. Stir.

Transfer curd to a nonmetal bowl and cover with plastic wrap, pressing wrap over the top of the curd to prevent skin from forming. Chill in refrigerator 30 minutes. Store in fridge up to one week, or spread on cooled tart shell and chill an additional 20 minutes before serving.

39. Flourless Cinnamon-Pecan Cookies

These tasty morsels are so packed with goodness and so filling, I never have to worry about eating too many.

Prep Time: 5 minutes

Cook Time: 10 minutes

Total Time: 15 minutes

Serves: 10 cookies

Ingredients:

2 cups raw pecans

½ teaspoons cinnamon

10 pitted dates, soaked in water for 15 minutes and drained

½ teaspoon sea salt

Preheat oven to 350°. Combine all ingredients in food processor and mix until a dough forms. Using a cookie scoop, form into balls and place on a *lined* baking sheet.

Bake for *10* minutes. Remove and cool completely before removing.

Can be stored in airtight *container* in the fridge for a couple of weeks. Or freeze for up to six months.

Conclusion

Thank you again for downloading this book!

I hope this book was able to give you all the whole food recipes that you'll need to succeed with the Whole food diet.

The next step is to start using some of these recipes and telling me how you liked them.

You can leave your comment in your review, and I'll make sure to read it!

Thank you and good luck!

Check out another book by Sheila Brown